Trucks

KU-213-167

Paul Stickland

MATHEW PRICE LIMITED

Two flatbed trucks. The green one is
delivering pipes to a building site.

The yellow one is on its way back
to reload.

A FLATBED TRUCK *is easy to load and unload. Sometimes the back has sides to keep the load safely.*

Whatever the load, it has to be safely strapped down. If anything fell off, it could cause an accident.

STRAPS

STRIPES *to warn any cars following behind.*

REAR WHEELS: *instead of two, trucks usually have four. This spreads the load and protects the tyres.*

The driver's seat is above the engine. This gives more space for carrying things.

Trucks have strong brakes.

CAB

Airflow to the engine is controlled by a GRILLE.

HEAD LIGHTS

FOG LIGHTS

DIESEL TANK

The engine has to be powerful enough to pull heavy loads up steep hills. When trucks have no load, they can go very fast.

A builder's truck has a special crane for loading and unloading bricks.

The driver controls the hydraulic arm with LEVERS.

This FLATBED TRUCK *has ten wheels. The power from the engine is delivered to all eight rear wheels, allowing it to drive onto bumpy and muddy sites.*

The HYDRAULIC CRANE *is powered by the same engine as the truck. The pistons move in and out.*

CRANE — HYDRAULIC ARM

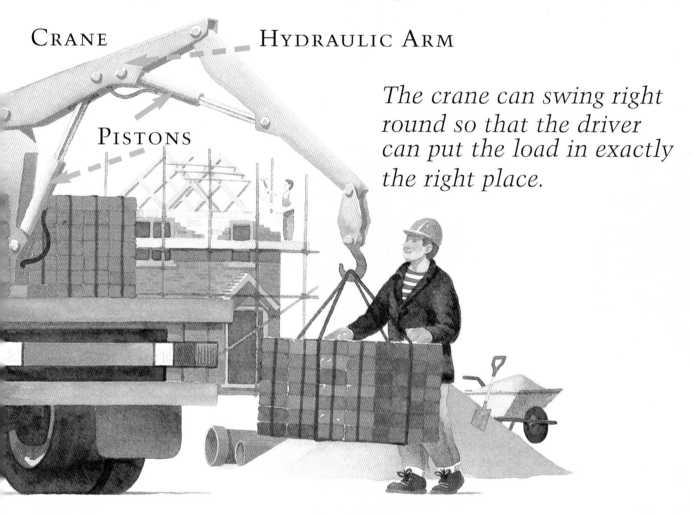

PISTONS

The crane can swing right round so that the driver can put the load in exactly the right place.

A strong hydraulic crane makes loading and unloading easy. It saves a lot of time and can lift very heavy weights like these bricks.

This truck has broken down.

The breakdown truck has arrived to
tow it to a garage.

WIRES *connect electricity from cab to rear.*

The whole cab tilts forwards to allow the mechanic to inspect and repair the engine.

CAB

REAR LIGHTS

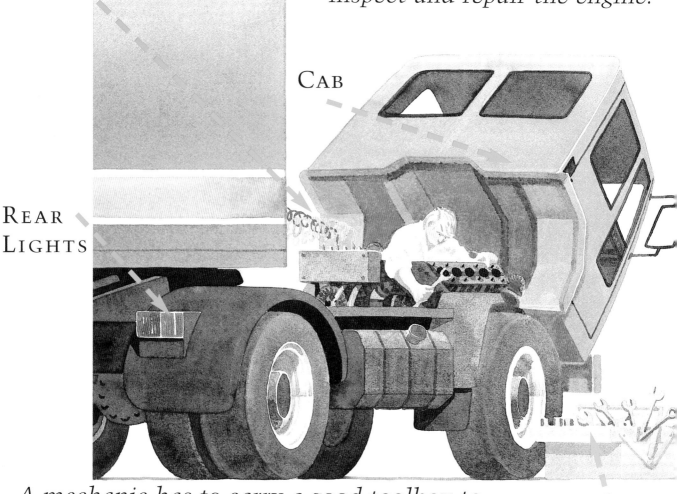

A mechanic has to carry a good toolbox to repair a truck on the road. Mechanics have to know how to take all sorts of different engines to pieces and then put them back together.

TOOLBOX

The crane can lift the truck free. A hook at the end of a thick cable will be used to tow the truck.

FLASHING LIGHTS warn other drivers whilst the road is cleared.

MIRRORS are on extended arms, so the driver can see the back of the truck.

HOOK

STEPS *up to the cab.*

STRIPES

Bright stripes make this powerful BREAKDOWN TRUCK easily seen by cars speeding past. This is necessary to avoid accidents. It can be very dangerous to pick up broken-down trucks in heavy traffic.

The tanker fills the garage's tanks as the

red lorry gets petrol from the pump.

The TANKER delivers petrol to the garages from the oil companies. It is stored in huge tanks underground.

See how much fuel you're loading from the DISPLAY.

CONTROL
PANEL

HOSEPIPE

Petrol has to be handled carefully, it explodes very easily. It is pumped out of the tanker through big hoses, which are carefully joined together to prevent leaks.

The top of this cab has been shaped to help push air over the lorry when moving along. This saves fuel.

CAB

FUEL
CAP

Diesel engines have enormous pulling power and use less fuel than petrol engines. But they still use a lot of fuel and need very large tanks to travel long distances.

Container lorries drive huge distances,

taking goods direct from ship to warehouse.

REFRIGERATED CONTAINER
TRUCK: *it keeps food fresh
while it travels long
distances, sometimes from
the other side of the world.*

*Air to cool or chill the
contents of the container
comes through this
GRILLE.*

*The owners of these big rigs are called truckers,
they spend most of their lives driving their trucks,
keeping them beautifully painted and polished.*

TANKS *contain compressed air for the air brakes.*

Truckers love shiny metal lights, air horns and accessories.

AIR HORNS

FOG LIGHTS

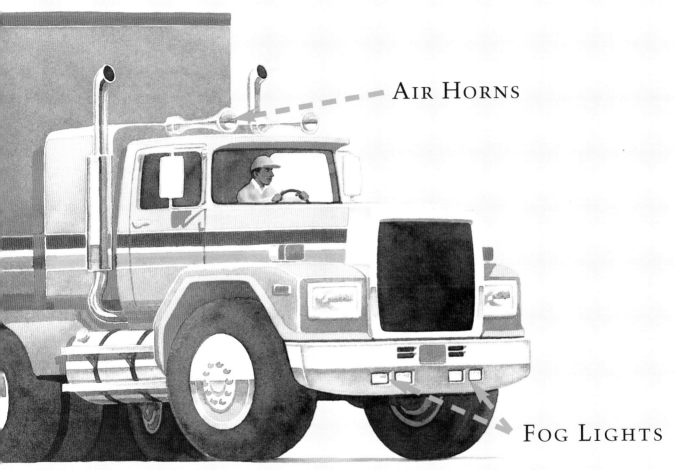

These ARTICULATED TRUCKS *have ten wheels: two at the front under the cab and eight at the rear, supporting the container. The front wheels on the cab section can swivel and pull the container round tight corners.*

What has the driver forgotten? What does he need to do before he gets to a road?

What is being carried? How would the driver get these off?

What is special about this tailgate?

How does the driver empty this load?

What is this cab doing without a container?

Why is this truck called a road train?

The **Answers** Page

He's forgotten to get the straps to tie the lumber down.

The back tips up and the tailgate opens.

These are beer barrels. He would use a fork lift truck or a crane.

The cab is racing. It can go very fast because it doesn't have a heavy load to pull.

The tailgate goes up and down to help load and unload the boxes.

It is called a road train because, like a train, it has another section hitched to it.

Copyright © Paul Stickland 1992, 2004

This edition first published in the UK 2004 by Mathew Price Limited The Old Glove Factory, Bristol Road Sherborne, Dorset DT9 4HP, UK

Designed by Douglas Martin
Printed in China
ISBN 1-84248-113-4